Battle Angel Alita Deluxe Edition Volume 3 copyright © 2013 Yukito Kishiro
English translation copyright © 2018 Yukito Kishito

Published in the United States by Kodansha Comics,
an imprint of Kodansha USA Publishing, LLC, New York.

Publication rights for this English edition arranged through Kodansha Ltd., Tokyo.

First published in Japan in 2013 by Kodansha Ltd., Tokyo, as
Gunnm, volumes 5 and 6.

ISBN 978-1-63236-600-9

Printed in China.

www.kodanshacomics.com

9 8 7 6 5 4 3 2 1

Translation: Stephen Paul
Lettering: Scott O. Brown
Editing: Ajani Oloye
Kodansha Comics edition cover design: Phil Balsman

THE GHOST IN THE SHELL
攻殻機動隊
DELUXE EDITION

THE DEFINITIVE VERSION OF THE GREATEST CYBERPUNK MANGA OF ALL TIME! THE PULSE-POUNDING CLASSIC OF SPECULATIVE SCIENCE FICTION RETURNS IN AN ALL-NEW HARDCOVER EDITION SUPERVISED BY CREATOR SHIROW MASAMUNE. THE THREE ORIGINAL *THE GHOST IN THE SHELL* VOLUMES ARE PRESENTED FOR THE FIRST TIME IN THE ORIGINAL RIGHT-TO-LEFT READING FORMAT, WITH UNALTERED JAPANESE ART AND SOUND EFFECTS.

KC
KODANSHA COMICS

SHIROW MASAMUNE
士郎正宗

NOW A MAJOR MOTION PICTURE!

THE SPACE OPERA MASTERPIECE FROM MANGA LEGEND LEIJI MATSUMOTO AVAILABLE FOR THE FIRST TIME IN ENGLISH!

LEIJI MATSUMOTO'S

Queen Emeraldas

KC
KODANSHA
COMICS

"If you like space cowboys and pirates or simply want to get lost in a strange dreamlike story, Kodansha's beautiful hardcover is worth checking out."
— Anime News Network

"It's not so much a manga as it is a song. But you'll want to listen to it again and again."
— A Case for Suitable Treatment

OTOMO
大 友 克 洋

A GLOBAL TRIBUTE TO THE MIND BEHIND AKIRA

A celebration of manga legend Katsuhiro Otomo from more than 80
world-renowned fine artists and comics legends
With contributions from:
- Stan Sakai
- Tomer and Asaf Hanuka
- Sara Pichelli
- Range Murata
- Aleksi Briclot
And more!
168 pages of stunning, full-color art

The Black Museum — The Ghost and the Lady

By Kazuhiro Fujita

Deep in Scotland Yard in London sits an evidence room dedicated to the greatest mysteries of British history. In this "Black Museum" sits a misshapen hunk of lead—two bullets fused together—the key to a wartime encounter between Florence Nightingale, the mother of modern nursing, and a supernatural Man in Grey. This story is unknown to most scholars of history, but a special guest of the museum will tell the tale of The Ghost and the Lady...

Praise for Kazuhiro Fujita's *Ushio and Tora*

"A charming revival that combines a classic look with modern depth and pacing... **Essential viewing both for curmudgeons and new fans alike.**" — Anime News Network

"**GREAT!** The first episode of Ushio and Tora captures the essence of '90s anime." — IGN

ALITA
Battle Angel ALITA
Last Order

The Cyberpunk Legend is Back!

In deluxe omnibus editions of 600+ pages, including ALL-NEW original stories by Alita creator Yukito Kishiro!

KC
KODANSHA

A new series from Yoshitoki Oima, creator of The New York Times bestselling manga and Eisner Award nominee *A Silent Voice*!

An intimate, emotional drama and an epic story spanning time and space...

TO YOUR ETERNITY

An orb was cast unto the earth. After metamorphosing into a wolf, It joins a boy on his bleak journey to find his tribe. Ever learning, It transcends death, even when those around It cannot...

THE TRUTH OF THE WALL!

DSHHH

THE HYDRO WALL! NO SMUGGLER HAS EVER MADE IT THROUGH THIS WALL SUCCESSFULLY...

CRAK

UNNGH!

CRUNK

THE WATER IS SO POWERFUL, EVEN ARMORED VEHICLES GET FLATTENED.

KABOOM

NOW! GO THROUGH!

EVEN IF YOU BLOW A HOLE IN IT WITH DYNAMITE...

BLUB

GWAAH!!

BLUB

...IT'LL JUST GO RIGHT BACK TO NORMAL.

THAT'S THE THIRD WAN THIS MOHNING!

AND THEN YOU'LL CYCLE THROUGH THE WALL FOR ETERNITY.

DSSHH

THE END.

YUKITO. 1993. 11. 21.

THE FARMS

FARMS WORKING DIRECTLY UNDER THE FACTORY. EACH STATION IS OVERSEEN BY A DECKMAN. IN ADDITION TO THE FACTORY ARMY, THE FARMS ARE PROTECTED FROM EXTERNAL ENEMIES BY CIVILIAN VIGILANTE GUARDS. WHILE FOOD IS PLENTIFUL ON THE FARMS, DOCTORS, AND CYBORG AND MEDICAL SUPPLIES ARE IN SHORT SUPPLY, MEANING THEY ARE RELIANT ON THE SCRAPYARD FOR HELP.

FACTORY RAIL

CHUGGA

CHUGGA

CHUGGA

CHUGGA

CHUGGA

CHUGGA

STATION GATES

1010

CIVILIAN CARA

FACTORY-OW

THERE ARE ELEVEN IN TOTAL, EACH UNDER FACTORY JURISDICTION. DUE TO ANTI-TERRORISM MEASURES, THE CUSTOMS CHECKS ARE QUITE SEVERE. THIS IS THE RELAY ROUTE VECTOR USED TO LURE YUGO INTO WORKING FOR HIM.

AIIIE!

NO, ZAPAN!!

STOP IT!

!!

HUFF!

HUFF!

AH...

EEEP!

SPLOTCH

SAR-AH...

OH NO... WHAT HAVE I...?

OH...

SARAH...

ZZT

ZAPAN

Former Hunter-Warrior:
Wanted for murder
50,000 chip bounty
Note: Injured face

Two years later

Bar New Kansas

HAH! IF YOU THINK ABOUT IT, RHYTHM AND MELODY ARE IMPORTANT IN BOTH MUSIC *AND* BATTLE...

ALL THIS TIME YOU HAD ME THINKING YOU WERE JUST A FIGHTER, BUT THERE WAS A SENSITIVE MUSICIAN UNDERNEATH!

BRAVO, BRAVO!

CLAP CLAP CLAP CLAP

IT'S *GREAT!* KNOW WHAT I'M TACKLING NOW?

HOW'S LIVING ON YOUR OWN TREATING YOU?

THANKS! TAKE CARE, GUYS!

WE'RE GONNA HEAD OUT AND DO SOME HUNTING!

HEY, *AWESOME* SET, ALITA!

DON'T LEAVE

NEVER HEARD OF HIM.

ANCIENT LITERATURE! ARE YOU FAMILIAR WITH HANS HENNY JAHNN*?

I'D GUESS IT'S ABOUT THE *YOU-KNOW-WHAT...*

WHAT DOES HE WANT?

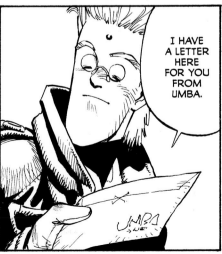

I HAVE A LETTER HERE FOR YOU FROM UMBA.

UMBA

*Hans Henny Jahnn: 1894-1959. The "great unknown German playwright." His signature work is *Thirteen Uncanny Stories*.

16

As for me, my new engineering company with Mr. Thompson is comin' along fine and dandy.

How ya doin', Alita?

It's about your old body (the Berserker) that you left in storage in your motorball days. You know, the one that Ed sold for cash without tellin' anyone...

You can probably guess why I'm writing you this letter...

So I hired some folks to track down where that Berserker body's been since then...

I'm guessin' he did that because he didn't want you to quit motorball an' go back to yer old life... but that never sat right with me.

17

THAT THING IS FAR TOO DANGEROUS... WE HAVE TO GET IT BACK JUST TO KEEP IT FROM FALLING INTO THE WRONG HANDS.

IT SAYS HE FOUND OUT WHO THE LAST PERSON TO BUY THE BERSERKER BODY WAS!

...but he's a real eccentric, and he won't even entertain a discussion...

I sent someone to this guy's house to negotiate a purchase on at least three occasions...

DESTY NOVA...

IT'S HIM...

IT SAYS HE'S A DOCTOR NAMED DESTY NOVA. AND UMBA INCLUDED THE ADDRESS, TOO.

18

WELL, WE'VE NEVER MET BEFORE...BUT I'VE ALWAYS WANTED THE CHANCE TO TALK TO HIM.

DO YOU KNOW HIM?

I'LL JOIN YOU.

I'M GOING TO GO VISIT THIS MAN AND BUY THE BODY BACK.

THAT SETTLES IT.

I'D RATHER NOT COMPLICATE MATTERS... JUST LET ME HANDLE THIS ONE.

YOU GIRLS STAY HERE AND GUARD THE HOUSE!!

KOHMI GA-GO!

SHUMIRA WILL GO, TOO!

BOOM

NI

AAAH...!

THWAM

FWUP

SINCE WHEN... DID YOU TURN INTO ALITA'S LITTLE LAPDOGS...?

HRRR!

HRRR!

HRRR!

CRAK

UNGF!

GONK

IS...IS THAT YOU, ZAPAN?!

W-WAIT... ZAPAN?

D-DO YOU STILL HOLD A GRUDGE OVER WHAT ALITA DID TO YOU?!

HNNNGG

WH-WHY ARE YOU DOING THIS...?

WHY, I'M TOUCHED... YOU RECOGNIZE ME.

DO YOU REMEMBER... WHAT SHE TOOK FROM ME? YOU'D BETTER...

OH, I DO... DON'T YOU REMEMBER WHAT HAPPENED?

TWITCH

YOU REALLY THINK YOU'VE GOT THE STRENGTH... TO OVERPOWER ALITA...?

HA HA HA... YOU'RE CRAZY, MAN...

IT WON'T END LIKE THIS...

SWING

I'VE GOT TO MAKE SURE SHE GETS A TASTE OF THE SAME HELL I'VE BEEN THROUGH...

THE REST OF US ARE NOTHING BUT INSECTS UNDER HER BOOT!

HEH HEH HEH!

SHE'S UNBELIEVABLE... WHO DO YOU THINK KILLED THAT MONSTER MAKAKU?!

AAAAH!

SHE WENT OVER TO THE WESTERN SECTOR AND COMPLETELY CONQUERED THE ENTIRE SPORT OF MOTORBALL!

RRRGH...!

RATTLE RATTLE

BRRR

THAT'S RIGHT! AND SHE'S FAR MORE POWERFUL THAN A MISERABLE CAST-OFF LIKE YOU!

SHE'S A DEMON! A DEVIL!!

DIE, YOU PSYCHO!

NOW'S MY CHANCE!

CHKING

AH...
AH...

ZM\\F

I NEED
STRENGTH
...

SARAH...

GIVE ME THE
STRENGTH
TO KILL THE
DEVIL...

FIGHT_024 Dog Master

ZAPAN'S BACK IN TOWN!

IT'S ZAPAN...

IT'S AN ACT OF VENGEANCE...

WH-WH-WHAT SHOULD WE DO?!

LOOK, THAT'S HIS BLADE, RIGHT THERE!

WHAT?

MOVE IT, YOUNG FELLA.

HUF!

HUF!

HUF!

LOOM

NO FEAR FOR OLD FRIENDS! YOU GOT THAT?!

WHAT *ELSE* WOULD WE DO? WE'RE HUNTER-WARRIORS, AND HE'S A MARK! WE KILL HIM!

PHEWWW

GRRR

ガルッ!!
GROWF
ウウッ
RRRR

LISTEN, THIS IS OUR TURF, YOU GOT THAT? FIND SOME- WHERE ELSE TO WORK!!

HUH?! WHADDA YOU WANT, GRAMPA?! YOU A HUNTER OR SOME- THING?!

シュ
SHING
!!

WHOA!

SNIF
SNIF
SNIF
SNIF

TAKE IT EASY!

28

B-BUT, ALITA...

YOU GOTTA KNOCK IT OFF WITH THIS "TURF" NONSENSE!

I HAVE A HUNCH...THAT ZAPAN'S ONLY AFTER ME.

...

I CAN CLEAN UP MY OWN MESSES.

HOW ABOUT THIS, SWEETIE? IT'S CALLED *PAINKILLER*, BUT WHAT IT REALLY DOES IS SEND YOU UP TO THE CLOUDS, MM-HMM.

...DRUGS...

NEED SOMETHIN'... TO TAKE THE FEAR AWAY...

THEN YOU WANT THIS ONE! *RAM IT DOWN* WILL FILL YOUR MIND WITH THE MOST EXQUISITE VISIONS!

RATTLE RATTLE

NO... I WANT A DRUG THAT WILL KILL SADNESS...

AH...AH... *NO!*

HANG ON, SWEETHEART, WHAT'S THAT YOU'VE GOT THERE? LET ME SEE IT!!

OOH!

CUT ME...A DEAL...

OH, NO, BABY! THIS IS ALL YOU GOT? YOU CAN'T FLY FOR THIS CHEAP!

30

CARE TO MAKE A LITTLE SWAP FOR WHAT YOU NEED?

G-GIVE HER... BACK...

JUST BETWEEN YOU AND ME, THE ONLY THING THAT GETS ME GOING THESE DAYS IS A WOMAN'S CADAVER...

WHY, SHE'S SIMPLY *GOR-GEOUS!*

OH, IT'S *TRÈS GHASTLY! WHAT A PIECE!!*

EEK...!

WHAM

SPLURT

KRUNCH

WHAM

WHAM

KRUSH

WHAM

SPLAT

WHAM

GONK

GONK

CRMBL

CRMBL

PHEWWW...

I'M JUST YOUR GARDEN-VARIETY LOSER...

CLIK

I DESERVE TO DIE LIKE THIS, SARAH...

...YOU TRIED TO HELP ME... TO SAVE ME...

AND YET...FOR SOME REASON...

...THE SAME WAY MY FATHER DOES..."

"YOU THINK...

WHY DID YOU HAVE TO DO THAT?!

"HE SAID THAT A LOSER DOESN'T NEED SYMPATHY..."

"BUT IN THE MISERABLE SCRAPYARD, COULD YOU REALLY CALL ANYONE A WINNER?"

AND SO...YOU GAVE UP YOUR OWN FLESH AND BLOOD TO FULFILL THAT GOAL.

"SO I FEEL LIKE MY MISSION IN LIFE IS TO BRING SOME HAPPINESS, HOWEVER SMALL, TO AS MANY PEOPLE AS I CAN."

HAH...WHAT A WHORE YOU WERE.

BUT I WON'T FOR-GIVE YOU!

NEVER FOR-GET!! NEVER FOR-GIVE!!

GYA HA HA HA HA!

"I WAS HAPPY TO HAVE YOU CUT OFF MY HEAD. I HAVE NO REGRETS."

I'M SURE THAT IF I COULD TALK TO YOU RIGHT NOW, YOU'D SAY...

HEH... HEH-HEH...

...

PARDON ME...

...BUT YOU'RE MURDOCK THE "DOG-MASTER," RIGHT?

BAR NEW KANSAS

HMPH.

YOU BET HE IS! MURDOCK'S ONE OF THE GREATEST HUNTER-WARRIORS WHO EVER LIVED! HE WAS A MATCH FOR OLD CLIVE LEE, THE "WHITE-HEAT PALM" MASTER WHO DIED FROM A LIGHTNING STRIKE!

OH? HE'S FAMOUS?

...

FANG! FAH-FAH! FAH-FAH!

TEP TEP TEP TEP

FAAAANG!!

WHY, AREN'T YOU SWEET!

GRIN

SORRY ABOUT THAT. EVER SINCE MY OLD MUTT DIED, SHE CALLS EVERY DOG SHE SEES "FANG"...

HE DOESN'T SEEM SO BAD...

HEH!

THAT WOMAN WAS MY DAUGHTER.

...WHEN ZAPAN KILLED THAT WOMAN AND WENT ON THE RUN...

...

TWO YEARS AGO...

35

...!!

IF SHE'D JUST LISTENED TO THE WISDOM OF HER DEAR OLD DAD, SHE WOULDN'T HAVE DIED SUCH A GRISLY DEATH.

SHE WAS QUITE A STUBBORN GIRL...

GLARE

...

ZAPAN'S BEEN ON THE RUN EVER SINCE, WITH HER HEAD IN TOW...

ZAPAN IS MINE!

YOU SEE WHAT I'M GETTIN' AT?

LOUD! GLORY! WINNER! FURY!

ACCEPT YOUR FATE, YOU DAMNED COCK-ROACH!

HMM?

WAIT, MURDOCK!

GRRRR

S-STAY BACK!

AIEE!

NO! HE'S MINE!!

...IT'S
OVER.

SLOSH

WHINE

WHINE

COME,
SARAH...
LET'S GO
HOME.

KBLOOSH

NO ONE
BOTHERS TO
SHED TEARS
FOR A
COWARD...

LOUD

FIGHT_025
Flask of Karma

SO IF THEY COME AT YOU WITH A KNIFE LIKE *THIS*, YOU BLOCK IT LIKE *THIS*.

YOU HOOK IT, THEN PUSH DOWN-WARD...

AND YOU'RE NOT GRABBING THE WRIST— YOU HAVE TO GET THE BASE OF THE THUMB!

THEN GRAB THE KNIFE HAND WITH YOUR LEFT.

...YOU SLICE HIS THROAT, AND YOU'RE DONE!

THEN YOU TWIST HIS WRIST TOWARD THE INSIDE, WHICH BREAKS THE KNIFE FREE...

NOW PRACTICE THIS ON YOUR OWN!

ANOTHER OPTION: YOU HOOK HIM AROUND THE NECK...

...THEN TOPPLE HIM TO THE GROUND, WHERE YOU CAN GIVE HIM THE BUSINESS!!

OH... THANK YOU.

WAN FOWER! FO YOU.

YES, YES, YOU *DO* HAVE FLOWERS.

WOBBLE ヨボ...

MISSER! I GAH FOWERS!

GUESS HE'S GONE SOFT, NOW THAT HE'S FINALLY AVENGED HIS DAUGHTER.

SENILE OLD COOT...

CAN'T BELIEVE THAT'S THE SAME OLD MAN WHO WAS JUST SHOOTIN' FLAMES OUTTA HIS EYES AT US.

WESSIN PEACE!!

MISSER'S DOTTA GWAVE!

FANG'S GWAVE!

WHOA!

TEK TEK TEK テテテ

Marker: Fang

50

...

PRESENT FROM IDO! SHUMIRA IS SO JEALOUS! SO JEALOUS!

IT'S FROM IDO? WHY DIDN'T HE GIVE IT TO ME HIMSELF?

ALITA!

I SEE... IT'S THREE YEARS TO THE DAY THAT IDO FOUND ME IN THE SCRAP PILES...

IDO...

BUT I CAN'T JUST TURN AROUND AND LEAVE...

ZSH

BZZZT!

THAT'S STRANGE. I WONDER IF HE'S NOT HOME...

...

I'M HERE TO FIND A WAY TO BUY BACK THE BERSERKER BODY.

I HAVE TO ADMIT, I'M CURIOUS TO FIND OUT WHAT HE'S LIKE.

THE MAN WHO OWNS THIS RESIDENCE, DESTY NOVA, IS APPARENTLY FROM ZALEM, JUST LIKE ME.

HE PERFORMED A BRAIN OPERATION ON JASUGUN...AND WAS MOST LIKELY RESPONSIBLE FOR MAKAKU, TOO.

HE SAVED BOTH OF THEIR LIVES...BUT I SENSE A KIND OF MALICE BEHIND HIS ACTIONS!

YOU MUST BE DESTY NOVA!

LET ME GUESS.

B-B-BOSS...

ZERRMPH

AND WHO ARE YOU? FROM ZALEM, I PRESUME?

THAT'S ME! I AM PROFESSOR DESTY NOVA.

I DIDN'T MEAN TO SNEAK INSIDE, I WAS JUST LOOK-ING FOR YOU.

CLANG

ER, ACTUALLY... I'M ONLY HERE TO BUY BACK THE BERSERKER BODY.

PLEASE, COME IN, COME IN, MY ZALEMITE FRIEND!

MY NAME IS IDO... DAISUKE IDO.

HOW DOES IT LOOK, ELI? ANY PROBLEMS?

ALLOW ME TO INTRODUCE MY LOVELY PARAMOUR AND ASSISTANT, ELI.

NONE, PROFESSOR. IT'S ALL SHIP-SHAPE.

OOOH, IT'S BEEN AWHILE SINCE I'VE SEEN A HANDSOME ORGANIC MAN.

WHAT'RE YOU UP TO TONIGHT?

COME WITH ME, YOU TWO.

KYA *HA HA!* SURPRISED? I DON'T BLAME YOU. THESE ARE ALL FAILURES.

WH- WHAT'S THIS?!

THEY'RE... THEY'RE INSANE.

EVERYTHING ONE MIGHT FIND ON THE SURFACE IS HERE—LOVE, HATRED, OPEN LUST, AND UNDENIABLE MADNESS...

BEING IN THIS ROOM FILLS ME WITH A SENSE OF PIETY, I ADMIT.

WH-WHAT IS THE TRUE PURPOSE OF YOUR RESEARCH, PROFESSOR NOVA?!

MY AREA OF EXPERTISE IS NANOTECH-NOLOGY*.

I REARRANGE MOLECULES IN WHICHEVER WAY I DESIRE TO CREATE IMPERCEPTIBLY TINY, LITTLE ROBOT SERVANTS.

BUT THAT IS ONLY THE MEANS.

THE MEANS TO WHAT END?!

BUT AGAIN, THAT IS ONLY THE MEANS!

I CAN CONTROL MY SERVANTS, ORDERING THEM TO RE-PAIR WOUNDS, TO SEVER AND REBUILD, TO MANAGE LIFE AND DEATH AUTONO-MOUSLY!

...IS THE END?!

AND WHAT...

*Nanotechnology: A nanomachine (hypothetically speaking) is named for being one nanometer in size, which is one billionth of a meter. The name was coined by Eric Drexler in 1986.

*Karma: The sum of activity, through actions, words, and thoughts, in terms of good and evil. Karma is said to influence the outcome of the events of one's life. The term is from Sanskrit, and means "action" or "deed."

YOU ACTUALLY *KNOW* THIS BRAIN?

WELL, ISN'T THIS A SURPRISE!

AAAGH!!

CRIKK

HUFF, HUFF... IT BELONGS TO A VICIOUS *KILLER!* IT MUST BE DE-STROYED!!

HE IS MY PATIENT.

I'M AFRAID THAT WON'T BE HAPPEN-ING.

AND AS OF NOW, SO ARE *YOU...*

KAAA! KOHMI DO! KOHMI DO!

"PLANT THREE SEEDS IN EACH INDIVIDUAL HOLE"...

GONZU!

WHATCHA DOIN' OVER THERE?

AAAH!

YOU GO BRING THE WATER AND A NEWSPAPER, KOYOMI!

OOOH.

IDO GAVE THEM TO ALITA AS A PRESENT!

WE'RE PLANTING FLOWER SEEDS.

THESE ONES ARE CALLED "SWEET PEAS."

HE SAID HE'D BE BACK BY LAST NIGHT, BUT I HAVEN'T HEARD A WORD FROM HIM SINCE HE LEFT.

I'M KIND OF WORRIED...

HE LEFT FOR THE NORTHERN SECTOR YESTERDAY. HE'S ON A SOLO MISSION TO BUY BACK THE BERSERKER BODY.

SPEAKING OF WHICH, I HAVEN'T SEEN HIM LATELY. WHAT'S HE DOING?

IN FLOWER LANGUAGE? UM, LET'S SEE...

IT SAYS, "KIND MEMORIES"!

HEY, ALITA! WHAT DOES "SWEET PEA" MEAN IN FLOWER LANGUAGE?

Book: How to Grow Flowers and Vegetables

HEY, ALITA! SOMEONE'S HERE FOR YOU!

KSHUNK

FLOWERS ARE A TREASURE WITHIN THE SCRAPYARD. TREAT THEM GENTLY.

THAT'S IDO, ALWAYS THE ROMANTIC.

71

CAR'S WAITING OUT FRONT.

IDO HIRED ME TO BRING YOU TO HIM.

SO YOU'RE ALITA?

UH, I HAVE TO GO PICK UP IDO NOW, HONEY. CAN YOU HANDLE THE REST?

WHA HAPPEN ALEETA?

SLOSH

DUNNO. I GOT HIRED OVER THE PHONE, THAT'S ALL I CAN TELL YOU.

D-DID SOMETHING HAPPEN TO HIM?!

I'M SORRY, MA'AM!

ALITA! HOW MANY TIMES HAVE I TOLD YOU NOT TO USE THE WINDOWS THAT WAY?!

F!! BOOM

JUST A MINUTE—I'LL BE RIGHT BACK!

K-THUMP

WHAP

PWOO!

I *TOLD* HIM I WANTED TO GO WITH HIM...

RUSTLE

STUPID, STUPID IDO...

DON'T WORRY, I'M COMING TO SAVE YOU...

LET'S GO!

SORRY!

ALITA!

IN THAT INSTANT, I FELT A MOMENTARY URGE TO STOP AND TURN BACK...

74

A SUDDEN WHIM CAUGHT ME, FILLING MY HEART WITH A RUSH OF SENTIMENT.

IT'S A RAINBOW!

Hee-hee!

I WAS GOING TO OPEN IT UP AND SAMPLE IT ONCE IDO GETS BACK.

HMM, THIS IS GOOD STUFF.

I'LL NEVER LET ANYONE HURT YOU!

I LOVE ALL OF YOU!

Meanwhile, at Desty Nova's residence, Northern Sector

WH-WHAT ARE YOU GOING TO DO TO ME?!

S-STOP! DON'T DO IT!

RATTLE RATTLE

NOTHING TO WORRY ABOUT. I'M ONLY INSTALLING ABOUT 10 MILLION RESTORERS* TO FIX YOU UP.

AAAH!

CALM YOUR- SELF DOWN, OR I'LL INJECT IT INTO YOUR EYEBALL INSTEAD.

*Restorer: A type of nanomachine that performs bodily repair on the cellular level. People with these nanobots in their body will have dramatically faster self-healing capabilities.

A GOOD FLAN ALWAYS CLEARS MY MIND!

YES, THERE'S NOTHING LIKE A GOOD BAKED *FLAN!*

OOOH...

JIGGLE *JIGGLE*

NUMMY!

CHOMP

THERE ARE TWO KINDS OF PEOPLE IN THE WORLD, IDO. THE GUINEA PIGS... AND THE EXPERIMENT-ERS WHO HAVE THE RIGHT TO USE THEIR SCALPELS ON THE FORMER.

ONCE YOU KNOW THE *SECRETS OF ZALEM*, YOU'LL CHANGE YOUR MIND...BUT I CAN'T BLAME YOU FOR NOT BEING READY YET.

SAY, IDO! ANY INTEREST IN BEING MY LAB ASSISTANT?

ABSOLUTELY NOT!

WE OUGHT TO GET THIS ALL SHIP-SHAPE BEFORE SHE ARRIVES.

AS A MATTER OF FACT, I'VE SUMMONED ALITA HERE. IT SHOULDN'T TAKE MORE THAN AN HOUR.

YOU *WHAT?!*

RRGH...

AND NOW, I OUGHT TO GIVE THIS BRAIN WHAT KARMA HAS DECREED IT DESERVES.

Y-YOU'RE GOING TO GIVE ZAPAN THE BERSERKER BODY!!

IT IS SUCH A TREMEN-DOUSLY ELEGANT PIECE OF MACHINERY.

KSHUNK

OH!

IT STEMS FROM THE SAME FOUNDATION OF NANO-TECHNOLOGY, BUT IT IS CONCEPTUALLY ALIEN TO MY WORK!

THIS SUIT IS LIKE ONE LIVING MACHINE!

ズルッ!! SHLUP

KYA-HA!

AND NOW, I SHALL UNLOCK THAT FUNCTION!

FOR WHATEVER REASON, THE MACHINE CELLS THAT MAKE UP THIS WETTZEUG HAVE A BUILT-IN PROGRAM THAT LIMITS THEIR ACTIVITIES.

TAP TAP TAP

DO YOU HAVE ANY IDEA WHAT MADNESS YOU'RE EMBARKING UPON?!

NO! STOP THIS!

OH, THE EXCITE-MENT! I SHIVER!

RATTLE RATTLE

MY GREATEST EXPERIMENT IS ABOUT TO BEGIN!

NO—THAT IS ITS TRUE FORM!

ズルッ ズルッ SHLUP

LOOK, PROFESSOR, IT'S MELTING!

GO GO

RMMBB

AAAAH!!

THE BERSERKERS WERE A CHAOTIC TOOL OF TERROR IN THE DAYS OF THE SPACE WARS— FIGHTERS SENT INTO ENEMY TERRITORY, PROGRAMMED TO INDISCRIMINATELY DESTROY AND MULTIPLY AT WILL ONCE GIVEN THE PROPER EXTERNAL COMMAND!!

Y-YOU *FOOL!* YOU'VE JUST ACTIVATED THE DORMANT BERSERKER MODE!

GRAB

Y-YES, MASTER!

BAZARD, CUT THE POWER! NOW!

BOOOM

KRAK

CRAK

LOOK OUT, PROFESSOR!

!

RATTLE

RATTLE

RGH!

KBOOM

AIEEE!

KSHUNK

CLANK

OKAY!

IDO! THAT CAPSULE CONTAINS A CELL-COLLAPSER CREATED FROM THE BERSERKER'S MACHINE CELLS!

INJECTING THEM IS THE ONLY WAY TO STOP IT!!

OH!

VWOM

AAAH!

MY FACE...

IT'S EVEN CAUSING BALL LIGHTNING*!

WHIF

WHIF

*Ball lightning: A mass of plasma that can form naturally in midair during thunderstorms.

PUTTER PUTTER PUTTER PUTTER PUTTER

HUP

ZMMF

HERE WE ARE.

RATTLE RATTLE

SKREEE

WH-WHAT'S THIS?!

IT'S BEEN MELTED AWAY INTO GLASS...

!

YOU MUST BE ALITA.

SADLY, IT SEEMS YOU'VE ARRIVED JUST A BIT TOO LATE...

I AM PROFESSOR DESTY NOVA.

NO! WAIT... WHERE'S IDO? WHAT HAPPENED TO HIM?!

WE ARE GOING TO LEAVE THIS TOWN NOW.

I'M A *GIRL*, DICK.

THANK YOU, BOY.

IDO...?

GLORY

IDO...WHAT HAPPENED TO IDO?!

THUNK

IDO...?

FIGHT_026 Collapse

UH...

...THIS BOX.

IDO IS IN...

AS I SAID...

WHAT DO YOU MEAN?

WH...

HEE HEE... くす くす‥

NOT A VERY BRIGHT GIRL, IS SHE?

CLIK

...

TAKE A LOOK FOR YOUR-SELF.

96

ドォォォォォ
KCHAK

L-
LIES!

THIS...
THIS
ISN'T
TRUE!

SHE'S
SUFFER-
ING FROM
ENDORPHIN
WITH-
DRAWAL*.

DOC?

...AH! HAHH!
HAHH! HAHH!
HAHH! HAHH!

*Endorphin withdrawal: When humans and other animals are around their close companions, their brains secrete endorphins that ease anxiety and produce happiness. When they feel separation from those companions, the brain stops producing endorphins, leading to a kind of chemical withdrawal. Some call this "love withdrawal."

NO, IT'S TRUE.

...IS DEAD.

IDO...

98

WHY...

FLOP

OH, I *LOVE* WATCHING PEOPLE FALL INTO MOURNING.

HEE HEE HEE...

IDO TRIED DESPERATELY TO STOP THE BERSERKER, BUT IT WAS IN VAIN...

SNORT

GO ON! CRY FOR ME!

?!

DSSHT

99

KBOON KBOON KBOON

KBOON

ARRGH!

WHA-?!

HYUMM

FACTORY 99

FACTORY LAW

ELIMINATION CONFIRMED! *BZZT!*

CLASS-A VIOLATION UNIDENTIFIED FLYING OBJECT* ELIMINATED!!

*Class-A violation UFO: All flying objects within Zalem airspace are shot down by the Netmen for Class-A crimes. This is why there are no birds in the Scrapyard.

KABOOM

VOOM

WHICH WAY'S THE KANSAS...?

BZZT.

FWOOO

N-NO...

BUT I...I
KILLED
YOU...

BUT THE LOSS OF SO MUCH BLOOD DOES MAKE ME FEEL RATHER UNWELL...

WE HAVE A HEALTHY STOCK OF RESTORER NANOBOTS IN OUR BODIES. THIS DAMAGE IS EASILY RECOVERABLE ON OUR OWN.

KOFF! KOFF!

HEH-HEH...

THE CHILL OF THAT METAL BLADE HURT SO GOOD.

!!

UNDERSTAND THAT I AM ABLE TO BRING IDO BACK TO LIFE!

IDO WARNED ME THAT YOU WERE IMPETUOUS, BUT I DIDN'T EXPECT AN ATTACK OUT OF NOWHERE...

BUT FOR NOW, CALM DOWN AND HEAR ME OUT!

IDO DIED WHEN HE ATTEMPTED TO STOP THE MAN NAMED ZAPAN*, WHO WAS BROUGHT BACK AS A BERSERKER.

FNUP

ZUERRCH

AAAAH!

WHOOOOSH

ZAP

ZAP

FWAP

ゴド!!
THUD

THE BERSERKER BODY IS BEING UTILIZED TO 120% OF ITS CAPACITY THANKS TO THE FORCE OF ZAPAN'S MADNESS!

THE BODY CAN BE SHAPED THROUGH ITS USER'S IMAGINATION, AND USING THAT TO PRODUCE AN ELECTROMAGNETIC EFFECT, ZAPAN CAN CREATE BALL LIGHTNING OF MANY THOUSANDS OF DEGREES KELVIN!

AND HE LIVES SOLELY FOR THE SAKE OF VENGEANCE AGAINST YOU, ALITA.

ZZSH

BAK

NEWKANSAS

ZAPAN IS... ALIVE?!

Z...

THERE CAN BE NO ESCAPE...

YOU ARE FATED TO FIGHT AGAINST ZAPAN.

BUT THERE'S NO FUN IN A BATTLE WITHOUT HOPE OF WINNING.

SO I WILL GIVE YOU A PRESENT, TO HELP YOU STAND A CHANCE.

CLUNK

...

IT WAS YOU WHO CREATED THAT MONSTER.

...FOR ZAPAN IS YOUR KARMA MADE FLESH.

THINK ABOUT IT HONESTLY, AND YOU'LL AGREE!

YANK

THIS SUB-STANCE IS CALLED "COLLAPS-ER."

YOU SAID YOU'D HEAL IDO!

THAT'S A PROMISE!!

IF YOU CAN INJECT THIS DEEP INTO THE BERSERKER BODY, YOU *MIGHT* STAND A CHANCE OF WINNING.

I'VE ALREADY TOLD HIM HE WAS MY PATIENT.

YES, HAVE NO FEAR.

OUCH!

SLIP

SNIFF

BWA HA HA!

SHUMIRA, GET THE PHONE!

OKAY, OKAY, OKAY!

GEH PHOW!

SHUMIRA CAN'T UNDER-STAND! CALL BREAKING UP!

DING!

SKRR
SKRR
...GET... HURRY...
...OM-ING...
SKRR
SKRR

HELLO! THIS IS THE KANSAS! WHAT CAN SHUMIRA DO FOR YOU?

ZAPAN IS BACK ALIVE, AND HE'LL BE COMING THERE IN SEARCH OF ME! PLEASE...

HURRY... HURRY, GET AWAY FROM THE KANSAS!

SURE THING.

HURRY, TAKE ME TO BAR KANSAS!!

BEEP, BEEP...

DAMN!

PUTTA

PUTTA

PUTTA

CAN IT...

CAN IT BE...

...MY FAULT...?!

IT WAS YOU WHO CREATED THAT MONSTER...

PLEASE, GOD...

PLEASE...JUST BE SAFE UNTIL I GET THERE, EVERYONE!

CLENCH!!

IF THE BERSERKER STARTS WREAKING HAVOC IN THE SCRAPYARD, ZALEM'S FORCES WILL BE FORCED TO INTERVENE SOONER OR LATER.

NO POINT IN STICKING AROUND...

AREN'T YOU GOING TO WATCH HOW THE EXPERIMENT TURNS OUT?

WELL, I SUPPOSE WE OUGHT TO LEAVE.

GONG GONG GONG GONG GONG

FASTER, FASTER!

WITH THIS HUNK OF JUNK?!

SKREEE

WELCOME!!

115

IS...
ALITA...

...HERE...?

MMM,
TOO BAD!
ALITA OUT
AT THE
MOMENT!

MR. GUEST
HERE TO
LISTEN TO
ALITA SING?

BOOOM

BZT

BZT

BAR NEW KAS

CLUNK

KRSSH

AA-AH!

BAM

EE-EI!

BAM

BAM

BLAM

BAR NEW

TK....

ZAMM

WHMM....

121

Y-YOU... YOU'RE ZAPAN?!

DROP DEAD AND GO... TO...

HEGH—

RATTLE RATTLE

HEEP!

HEEP!

AH... AAAH!

SPLAT

...IS ALITAAAA?

SWISH

SWISH

HEH!

HEH!

HEH!

AND WHERE...

HOW ABOUT A DRINK ON THE HOUSE?

H-HEY, SETTLE DOWN, PAL... NO TROUBLE FROM ME.

HFF

HFF

SAY, ZAPAN...

RATTLE
カチカチ

HERE, IT'S THE SAME BOTTLE OF GOOD STUFF YOU ALWAYS WANTED TO TRY.

...YOU REMEMBER THE PAST?

...

WHEN I NEEDED TO REBUILD THIS PLACE, YOU WERE THE ONE WHO RAISED THE MOST MONEY FOR THE CAUSE...

PROTECT THE CHILDREN, FURY.

TODAY I WILL FINALLY SEND YOU WHERE YOU BELONG!!

HEY, GRAMPS...

VWAAH!

I HAVE A DOG, TOO!

DOGS...

HEH HEH... DOGS.

TH-THE BALL LIGHTNING TURNED INTO A BEAST?!

BOOM

IT'S... A LEGENDARY *BLACK DOG*!!

RAAH

HA!

HA!

WINNER! GLORY! LOUD!

*Black dog: A supernatural monster from English folklore. It's known as the Black Shuck in Norfolk, a puca in Ireland, and the Gurt Dog in Somerset. It appears along with a bolt of lightning, kills people, then disappears in an explosion of light. It also leaves behind the stench of sulfur.

IT IS YOURSELF THAT YOU SEE IN ME.

WE BOTH LOVED SARA... AND WE BOTH POSSESSED SUCH INTENSE FEELINGS OF JEALOUSY AND INFERIORITY TOWARD HER THAT WE HARBORED A DEEP DESIRE TO KILL HER.

SO LET US HAVE OUR VENGEANCE ON ALITA TOGETHER!

AND IN ORDER TO EASE OUR SENSE OF GUILT, THERE IS A SIMPLE SOLUTION...

JUST ONE SCAPEGOAT*- ANYONE WILL DO.

I...I AM HER FATHER...

N-NO!

AND YOUR RAGE AT ME IS BECAUSE YOU ARE ENVIOUS THAT IT WAS I WHO DID THE DEED?

A SACRIFICE THAT WE MIGHT OFFER UP TO SARA'S GHOST...

EITHER WAY, WE ARE BIRDS OF A FEATHER...WE ARE SINNERS.

*Scapegoat: The term comes from ancient Israel, where a goat was cast out into the desert on a day of atonement, bearing the sins of the community as a sacrificial offering.

132

136

オオ OOOH

SHUMIRA... KOYOMI! I'M SO GLAD!

DON'T TOUCH THEM!

WHA...?

AND IT'S ALL BECAUSE OF **YOU!**

LOOK AT THIS! LOOK WHAT HAPPENED TO US...!

WINNER

Sign: Daisuke Ido Repairs • Cyborgs, Androids, Robots;
Repairs, Tuning & Maintenance for all models!

FIGHT_027 Scapegoat

KABOOOM ドゴゴォ!

SKREE

THEY DOIN' NIGHTTIME CON-STRUC-TION?!

GOOD GRIEF, WHAT'S WITH ALL THE RACKET?!

WHOA, WHAT'S GOING ON?!

FACTORY DEFENSE 01

ZDMM ズーン

AAAH!

TARGET ACQUIRED! AUTHORIZING USE OF ANTI-TERRORISM WEAPONS!

PREPARE TO ATTACK IN 2, 1...

142

145

WHOOOO

KRRSH

KRUNCH

HEH... IT'S ACTUALLY KINDA REFRESHING WHEN SHIT GETS THIS BUSTED UP.

ZAPAN IS YOUR KARMA MADE FLESH...

LOOK WHAT HAPPENED TO US!

AND IT'S ALL BECAUSE OF YOU!

PWUNK

147

NO, I...

EVERYBODY WAS JUST FINE BEFORE YOU CAME AROUND... EVEN ZAPAN!

YOU'RE A PESTILENCE, ALITA!

PLEASE, JUST... LEAVE US IN PEACE!

ALITA...

HERE...

SHUMIRA, FURY, LET'S GO...

GOTTA START OVER FROM NOTHING AGAIN.

...

148

THANK YOU, SHUMIRA.

IT WAS ALL THAT MONSTER MAN.

IT'S NOT ALITA'S FAULT.

...

...YOU'LL SEE HIM AGAIN SOMEDAY.

I'M SURE...

WHERE'S IDO...?

TAKE CARE...

SHU-MIRA!

149

SHLUK
SHLUK

ドッ
ドッ
BLUK

BLUK

ドッ
BLUK

I'M ALL
ALONE.

I'M
REALLY ALL
ALONE THIS
TIME...

...

SO HOW DID
THINGS TURN
OUT SO, SO
BAD...?

UP UNTIL
THIS POINT,
I'VE ALWAYS
GIVEN MY ALL
TO DO WHAT
WAS RIGHT.

WHEN YOU'RE SUPERIOR TO OTHER PEOPLE, IT JUST GETS 'EM HATIN' YOU.

WELL, THAT'S EASY.

IF THERE'S ANYTHING I HATE, IT'S PEOPLE WHO MOPE AROUND OVER STUFF THAT ALREADY *HAPPENED!*

LISTEN, I DON'T REALLY CARE, BUT KNOCK OFF THE GLOOM 'N DOOM.

HAH! ARE YOU *THAT* DENSE?

WHY?

HUMAN BEINGS ARE MEANT TO BE FREE, YOU GOT THAT?!

YOU PEOPLE WHO TIE YOUR-SELVES DOWN TO *RESPONSIBILITY* AND *GUILT* AND *DUTY* AND ALL THAT CRAP MAKE ME SICK!

WHAM

THE FACTORY TROOPS ARE ALL WIPED OUT... THE ONLY WAY FOR US TO CALM THE DEMON'S ANGER...

...IS FOR YOU TO BE A SACRIFICE!!

ALITAAA...

GRRROOOHHH!

THEY WOULD RATHER FIND A SUBSTITUTE THAT THEY CAN RELY UPON AND ABANDON TO CERTAIN DEATH.

WHY DO THEY ACCEPT IT, AND EVEN FIND SOLACE IN IT?

WHY DO THEY NOT FIGHT TO CONQUER THEIR WEAKNESS?

IS THIS HOW WEAK AND LOW THE HUMAN MIND CAN BE?

C'MON, ALITA!

FORGET THEM! WHO CARES WHAT THEY THINK?

AND I...

CLENCH

159

OHHH!

...!

> "The goat will carry on itself all their sins to
> a remote place; and the man shall release
> it in the wilderness."
> -Leviticus 16:22

162

164

I SAW MYSELF, WEAK-MINDED, TWISTED BY ENVY AND HATRED, MONSTROUS TO BEHOLD...AND I TREMBLED!

A BEAUTIFUL, MOURNFUL TUNE, THE LIKES OF WHICH I'D NEVER HEARD IN MY ENTIRE LIFE...

AND IN THAT MOMENT OF WEAKNESS, I HEARD A MELODY THAT PIERCED ME STRAIGHT TO MY CORE...

MY TERROR AND SENTIMENT MIXED TOGETHER, LEAVING ME HELPLESS TO CONTROL MYSELF...AND SO I BAWLED LIKE A CHILD...

I WAILED AND SOBBED!

ONCE I HAVE REDUCED YOU TO A BLOODY PULP...

ALITA...

THE BODY HAS A WILL OF ITS OWN, A WILL THAT DEMANDS DESTRUCTION... I CANNOT STOP IT! IT WILL ACT UNTIL I'VE DESTROYED THE ENTIRE TOWN...

...I WILL BE ERADICATED WITHOUT A TRACE, TORN OUT OF THIS ACCURSED BODY FROM THE INSIDE.

IT IS MY FINAL WISH, IN FACT!!

BUT THAT IS NO PROBLEM TO ME!

...

ド オ オ オ・・・・・！ *BOOOOM*

WHY AREN'T THE FACTORY AND THE HUNTER-WARRIORS DOING ANYTHING ABOUT THIS?!

PLEASE, ZALEM ABOVE...

UH-OH...THE DEMON'S ON AN-OTHER RAMPAGE.

NO, NO, NO!

DON'T BE AFRAID, SHUMIRA. IT'S VERY FAR AWAY. WE'RE SAFE HERE...

WAAAHHH...

HNGK!

SHUMIRA IS TIRED OF BEING A WEAK LITTLE CRYBABY!

SHNIFF

IT'S PATHETIC...

SHUMIRA DOESN'T HAVE THE BRAVERY TO BE A SACRIFICE FOR EVERYONE ELSE!

BUT ALITA IS FIGHTING ALL ON HER OWN FOR US...

...

YOU CAN START BY HELPING AT THE SOUP LINE TO FEED THE HUNGRY!

IN THAT CASE...WOULD YOU LIKE TO HELP OUT WITH OUR WORK? IT'S FOR A GOOD CAUSE!

177

AH! AH!

WHAK

WHAK

I SHALL BURY YOU UNDER THE EARTH, AND WITH YOU, MY SHAMEFUL PAST OF HUMILIATION.

THE GUN!!

GWOAA

FAREWELL, MY SIN! MY EVIL! MY EVERY REGRET!

WHAT?!

FURY

FIGHT_029
Lion and the Lamb

FIGHT_029
Lion and the Lamb

...!

HA HA!

HAAA HAAA HA HA HA!

HEH...

HEH HEH...

BUT I SHOT HIM WITH THE COLLAPSER!

SHWAP

RGH!

...THAT ZAPAN AND ALITA'S FIGHT SHOULD BE REACHING ITS CONCLUSION RIGHT ABOUT NOW.

I'D VENTURE TO SAY...

SNORT...

PROBABLY NOT... IF ANYTHING, IT'S ALL THEY CAN DO TO STAY ALIVE IN THE MOMENT.

HAS ANYONE EVER CONQUERED THEIR KARMA AFTER YOU TOLD THEM ABOUT IT, PROFESSOR

AND MY RESEARCH SHALL ETERNALLY STUDY HOW WE PROCESS THAT FACT AND COME TO GRIPS WITH IT!

AND YET STILL WE LIVE ON... OUR LIVES AND HISTORY ARE NOTHING BUT A LONG STRING OF DEVASTATING, IRREVERSIBLE MISTAKES.

KYA HA HA HA! BUT OF COURSE! YOU DO HAVE YOUR FETISHES, DON'T YOU?

OH, BUT DON'T MAKE HIM METAL, PLASTIC, OR RUBBER! HE OUGHT TO BE MADE OF REAL MEAT...

AND I FULLY INTEND TO! IDO WILL BE A NECESSARY ASSISTANT TO MY GREAT PROJECT!

BY THE WAY, PROFESSOR, YOU PROMISED HER THAT YOU WOULD BRING THIS MAN BACK TO LIFE...

191

WHAT'S
THE
MATTER,
ZAPAN?

FLAP

FLAP

PLISH

I HAD... THE MOST HORRIBLE DREAM...

I HAD NO HOPE LEFT... I KILLED SCORES OF PEOPLE... WHAT AN AWFUL NIGHTMARE...

THAT I MADE A MISTAKE AND KILLED YOU...AND THE KNOWLEDGE DROVE ME MAD. I TURNED INTO A MONSTER AND SWORE VENGEANCE ON EVERYTHING...

I'M SO, SO TERRIFIED. WHAT IF...WHAT IF I *LOST* YOU...?

SARAH...I'M WORRIED.

YOU'RE FINE... IT WAS JUST A DREAM. THAT'S NOT THE KIND OF PERSON YOU ARE.

TELL ME WHAT I SHOULD DO.

WHAT WOULD I DO, SARAH...?

DON'T BLAME ANYONE ELSE FOR YOUR TROUBLE... JUST FACE THE FACTS AND HOLD YOUR HEAD HIGH.

NO MATTER HOW HARD IT GETS...HOW MUCH YOU SUFFER...YOU MUST ACCEPT IT.

...DON'T TRY TO DENY IT. DON'T BE STUBBORN.

IF YOU MAKE A MISTAKE, AND KNOW DEEP DOWN THAT YOU'VE LOST...

YOUR VALUE IS NOT TIED TO WHAT YOU'VE WON AND LOST IN LIFE.

WHOOSH

NOT WITH
MY MEASLY,
PATHETIC
HEART...

KBOOM

KRRSH
ガラ
ガラ

FWOOM

I
CAN'T...

UH...
UH...

DRAGG!!

"IDO GAVE THEM TO ALITA AS A PRESENT!"

"WHATCHA DOIN' OVER THERE?"

"WE'RE PLANTING FLOWER SEEDS."

IT'S GROW-ING...

"IT SAYS, KIND MEMORIES!"

"IN FLOWER LANGUAGE? UM, LET'S SEE..."

Battle Angel Alita Part 5: Lost Sheep / END

Nanotechnology

EXPLAINED!

AS AN EXPERT IN THE FIELD, I SHALL BE PROVIDING A LESSON ON THE BASICS OF NANOTECH.

ONE NANOMETER IS 10^{-9} METERS, OR 1/1,000,000,000TH OF A METER. "NANO" COMES FROM THE GREEK ROOT NANOS, MEANING "DWARF." INCIDENTALLY, THE KANJI CORRESPONDING TO ONE NANO IS 塵, MEANING "DUST."

A NANOMACHINE IS A MICROSCOPIC ROBOT CONSISTING OF GEARS, BEARINGS AND MOTORS CONSTRUCTED AT THE INDIVIDUAL MOLECULAR LEVEL. IT'S POWERED BY STATIC ELECTRICITY, AND DUE TO THE PROPERTIES OF MOLECULAR BONDS, IS VERY HARDY. IT RUNS OFF OF PRELOADED PROGRAMMING. THESE MOLECULAR ROBOTS ARE CALLED "ASSEMBLERS."

20 nm

NOVA'S ASSEMBLER DESIGN. 20 NANOMETERS IS THE SIZE OF THE WORLD'S SMALLEST VIRUSES.

AN ASSEMBLER CAN GRAB AND PLACE MOLECULES AND ATOMS AT A SPEED OF A MILLION PER SECOND, MEANING THAT IT CAN CREATE A PERFECT REPLICA OF ITSELF IN ABOUT FIFTEEN MINUTES.

WHEN EACH COPY THEN REPEATS THE REPLICATION PROCESS, THEIR NUMBERS GROW EXPONENTIALLY. WITHIN TEN HOURS YOU'D HAVE 68 BILLION NANOMACHINES. IN LESS THAN A DAY, THEY'D WEIGH AN ACTUAL TON. BY THE END OF TWO DAYS, THEY COULD WEIGH MORE THAN THE ACTUAL EARTH. NATURALLY, THERE WILL BE MULTIPLE LAYERS OF PROGRAMMING AND FAILSAFE MECHANISMS DESIGNED TO AVOID SUCH A DISASTER.

THE ROOTS OF NANOTECHNOLOGY

1942: THE FIRST PIECE OF SCI-FI WRITING INVOLVING NANOTECH: ROBERT A. HEINLEIN'S SHORT STORY "WALDO."

1959: RICHARD FEYNMAN GIVES A LECTURE TITLED "THERE'S PLENTY OF ROOM AT THE BOTTOM."

1976: ERIC DREXLER FIRST PROPOSES THE CONCEPT OF THE "ASSEMBLER."

1981: THE STM (SCANNING TUNNELING MICRO SCOPE) IS DEVELOPED BY DRS. ROHRER AND BINNIG AT IBM ZURICH RESEARCH LABORATORY.

1986: ERIC DREXLER'S BIBLE OF NANOTECHNOLOGY: ENGINES OF CREATION.

1990: IBM SCIENTISTS USE THEIR STM TO CREATE THE IBM LOGO USING ATOMS (VISUALIZED BELOW).

5 nm — SPELLED USING 35 XENON ATOMS.

THE CREATION OF FLAN!

SHLOP

HEH HEH... WITNESS THE BRILLIANCE OF MY FLAN MACHINE!

YOU JUST SHOVEL IN WATER, MUD, FISH BONES, AND WHATEVER ELSE YOU HAVE ON HAND, AND...

IN THEORY, ASSEMBLERS CAN ESSENTIALLY CREATE ANYTHING THAT IS PHYSICALLY POSSIBLE TO EXIST. THEIR INDUSTRIAL POWER IS BASICALLY LIMITLESS.

IN PRACTICE

JIGGLE

IT'S A NANO-MIRACLE! THE BIRTH OF GLORIOUS FLAN!

YAY!

- BRAIN RECONSTRUCTION........(BRAIN AUGMENTATION)

- BERSERKER BODY...........................(MECHANICAL LIFE)

- ARTIFICIAL SPINE...............(ARTIFICIAL STRUCTURES)

- RESTORERS...(IMMORTALITY)

NUMMY!!

(OTHER USES)

- SYTHESIZING FOOD FROM INORGANIC MATTER
- AUTO-GROWTH/COMPLETION OF ALL KINDS OF MECHANICAL DEVICES
- DEVELOPMENT OF NEW MATERIALS
- MOLECULAR COMPUTING
- PLANET TERRAFORMING
- ETC.

THEN THE MACHINE WENT ON THE FRITZ.

JIGGLE

JIGGLE

JIGGLE

AAAH!

RMMBB

THE ASSEMBLERS WENT COMPLETELY OUT OF CONTROL AND TRANSFORMED NOVA'S ENTIRE LAB INTO A GIANT MASS OF FLANS.

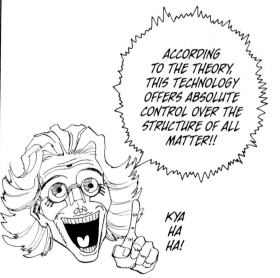

ACCORDING TO THE THEORY, THIS TECHNOLOGY OFFERS ABSOLUTE CONTROL OVER THE STRUCTURE OF ALL MATTER!!

KYA HA HA!

THE END.

YUKITO.
1993. 8. 12.

Big Generator, page 15

The lyrics to Alita's song in this scene come from the original English adaptation of the Battle Angel Alita manga by Fred Burke and Toshifumi Yoshida for Viz Media in 1998, and are printed as such in the latest edition of the manga in Japan. However, in the initial 1993 Japanese release, she was singing the lyrics (with proper attribution) to the Yes song "Big Generator." Some remnants of this can be seen in the crowd chants, which are left in their untouched state like all of the sound effects in this edition.

Flower language, page 71

Originally called *hanakotoba* in Japanese, flower language is a way to communicate meaning through flowers. In the West, this can be called "the language of flowers" or "florigraphy." In Japan, *hanakotoba* as a concept is fairly common, so it often comes up in media like manga and anime.

RAIN MAKER

BATTLE
ANGEL ALITA

PART 6

PRESENTED BY YUKITO KISHIRO

CONTENTS

FIGHT_030 Judgment Day

HUH...?

220

YOUR ACTUAL BODY IS INSIDE ONE OF THE FACTORY BUILDINGS.

OBSERVE!

OUR COMMAND TO HALT THE DISPOSER* WAS RECEIVED JUST IN TIME TO KEEP YOU FROM BEING ENTIRELY DESTROYED.

BUT IF LEFT UNADDRESSED, YOUR BRAIN CELLS WILL PERISH WITHIN A MATTER OF HOURS...

WH-WHAT IS THIS? WHY ARE YOU SHOWING ME THIS...?

WHAT DO YOU WANT?!

...

IN OTHER WORDS, YOU ARE DYING IN THE REAL WORLD.

221

*Disposer: An electric waste-disposal machine that crushes garbage and flushes it into the sewers.

AND IN EXCHANGE?

I CAN GIVE YOU A NEW BODY AND A NEW LIFE.

I WILL HAVE YOUR CLASS-A CRIMINAL SENTENCE ANNULLED.

I WILL SPARE YOUR LIFE.

HMPH!

YOU WILL WORK IN THE SERVICE OF ZALEM.

UWEEE

THIS WOULD BE A SPECIAL DUTY, SOMETHING THAT THE DECKMEN CANNOT HANDLE.

HRM...

MWAH?

NOT IF YOU'RE GOING TO TURN ME INTO A DECKMAN!

222

WE HAVE BEEN MONITORING YOUR ACTIONS OVER THE LAST TWO YEARS THROUGH THIS TR-55'S EYE.

K- KIMJI ?!

WE SENT A THOUSAND ARTIFICIAL TR-55 LIFEFORMS TO THE SURFACE TO LOOK FOR POTENTIAL PERSONNEL FOR OUR PROJECT.

AND WE PLACE AN EXTREMELY HIGH VALUE ON YOUR FIGHTING ABILITIES!

OH, NO... SO KIMJI WAS JUST KEEPING TABS ON ME ALL ALONG...?

223

BUT DREAMS DO NOT LAST LONG.

...THEN OPEN THAT YELLOW DOOR AND PROCEED OUTSIDE!

IF YOU TRUST ME, AND HAVE THE COURAGE TO RETURN TO REALITY...

...IF...IF I DECIDE TO BECOME ZALEM'S TOOL...

OF COURSE.

...CAN I BECOME STRONGER?

YOU WILL RECEIVE THE GREATEST POSSIBLE ASSISTANCE FROM US IN TERMS OF INFORMATION, EQUIPMENT, AND MAINTENANCE.

YOU WILL BE CODENAMED *TUNED UNIT 1*, THE ULTIMATE EARTHBOUND AGENT OF ZALEM.

...BY THE NAME OF DESTY NOVA.

THE CURRENT MISSION OF OUR *TUNED* AGENTS IS TO CAPTURE AN ESCAPED ZALEMITE SCIENTIST...

DESTY NOVA ...?!

D...

THAT'S RIGHT. BEYOND THE YELLOW DOOR...

GRIN

...IS THE ONLY PLACE WHERE YOU WILL FIND YOUR FUTURE.

I JUST WANT TO SEE HOW FAR MY BELIEF IN MYSELF CAN CARRY ME.

SUMMONING UP ALL THE COURAGE I HAVE...

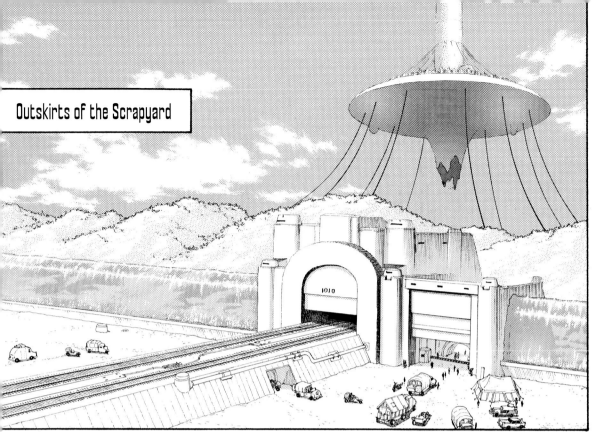

Outskirts of the Scrapyard

FIGHT_031 Angel of Death

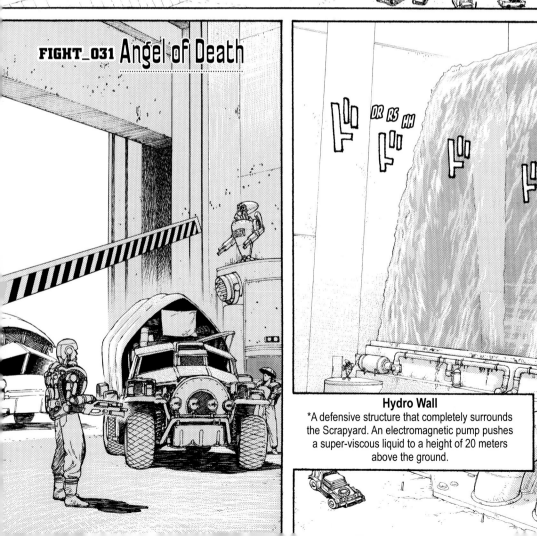

Hydro Wall
*A defensive structure that completely surrounds the Scrapyard. An electromagnetic pump pushes a super-viscous liquid to a height of 20 meters above the ground.

FIGHT_031 Angel of Death

Factory Rail
*A train system for ferrying cargo from farms and quarries to the Factory. It is literally a lifeline between Zalem and the Scrapyard. A pressurized water reactor is used for the locomotive's boiler.

WE USED TO HAVE A *DEAL* IN PLACE—AS LONG AS WE PAID THE BANDITS A TOLL, THEY WOULDN'T ATTACK OUR CARAVANS...

THAT'S FIVE CARAVANS WIPED OUT, INCLUDING ALL THEIR MERCENARY BODYGUARDS. WE'RE LOOKING AT LOSSES OF AT LEAST 40 MILLION CHIPS, MR. VECTOR.

THEY'RE NO JOKE... IN THE SOUTHERN SECTOR, THEY EVEN STOLE AN ENTIRE FACTORY TRAIN!!

...BUT EVER SINCE THOSE BARJACK MOBILE BANDITS SHOWED UP FIVE YEARS AGO, THEY'VE BEEN EXPANDING THEIR REACH AND MESSIN' UP MY ARRANGEMENT!

THE ONLY THING WE KNOW ABOUT THE LEADER OF BARJACK IS THE NAME *DEN*.

I CAN'T BELIEVE THEY'RE TRYING TO SCREW WITH THE FACTORY ITSELF! IF I DON'T GET A HANDLE ON THIS, THEY COULD MUSCLE ME OUTTA THE BROKERING MARKET.

242

IDIOTS... THEY HAVE NO IDEA WHAT THEY'RE GETTIN' INTO WITH BARJACK.

KEH... ALL THOSE HUNTER-WARRIORS FROM INSIDE THE SCRAPYARD. THEY EVER EVEN SHOT A GUN?

Helmet: Safety First

IN THAT CASE...

IS THAT SO?

SORRY, PAL. WE JUST FILLED ALL FOURTEEN SPOTS.

WHAP

KRAASH

I THINK YOU'VE GOT AN OPENING NOW.

D-03

ZWOOSH

*Naked: When used in this sense, a slang term that refers to being biological or unarmed; without cybernetic enhancements or weapons.

N-NAME'S *YORG.*

A-ASK ME ANYTHING YOU W-WANT. F-FIRST TRIP, RIGHT?

H-HEY, I S-SAW THAT FIGHT. IT WAS W-WILD! HEH HEH...

Y-YOU WANT MY LUNCH?

KCHAK

G-GOTTA FEEL UN-COMFORTABLE WITH YOUR G-GUN LIKE THIS. PUT IT IN B-B-BE-TWEEN YOUR SHOULDER BLADES... THERE.

AH, THANKS.

HEH HEH...

TH-THAT WAY, IF YOU TRY TO P-PRY IT OFF OR ESCAPE FROM THE T-TRAIN, YOUR HEAD GOES BOOM!

SEEMS AWFUL STRICT...

IT'S LIKE A D-DOG C-COLLAR. CAN'T TAKE OFF THE RENT-A-GUN DURING THE C-CONTRACT.

IT'S GOING TO BE A BOTHER WHEN I NEED TO TAKE A SHIT. CAN'T I RE-MOVE THE GUN?

EVER HEARD OF *B-BAR-JACK?*

R-RUMOR SAYS THEY FOUND A H-HUGE STOCK-PILE OF ANCIENT BUT P-POWERFUL WEAPONS IN SOME PRE-CENTURY RUINS...

M-MOST OF THE OLD G-GUARDS ALL GOT SPOOKED AND LEFT.

THEM BANDITS WHO STOLE A TRAIN OR SOMETHIN', RIGHT?

I'VE GOT MY W-WIFE AND KID WAIT-ING AT FARM 22, WHERE THIS T-TRAIN'S HEADING.

S-SEE?

WHY'D YOU STAY BEHIND?

I'M FIXIN' TO HEAD BACK HOME AFTER RAISING SOME CASH.

FAMILY.

THAT'S NICE.

ALONG THE SEA, OVER THE MOUNTAINS TO THE WEST.

OH? WH-WHERE YOU FROM?

HA HA! HA HA! I D-DON'T BLAME YA. THAT PLACE IS F-FULL OF CYBERS, MAN. AIN'T NO HOME FOR *PEOPLE.*

CAME UP TO THE SCRAPYARD A YEAR BACK, WANTIN' TO SEE ZALEM...BUT THE CITY LIFE DIDN'T SUIT ME. I'M SHIPPIN' OUT!

KOMBINAT LIFE

1G

VWOOOM

E-EVEN THE HEAD MERCENARY D-DOESN'T KNOW WHO SHE IS.

SHE DOESN'T HAVE A RENT-A-GUN ATTACHED. IS SHE NOT A HIRED MERCENARY?

Y-YOU DON'T WANNA MESS WITH HER.

H-HEY!

AND THAT IF YOU T-TALK TO HER, YOU'LL LOSE A YEAR OFF YOUR L-LIFE.

SHE SEEMS TO HAVE S-SOME KIND OF UNSAVORY CONNECTION TO THE F-FACTORY. EVERYONE BELIEVES SHE'S THE A-ANGEL OF DEATH.

HEY, CHIEF! WE GOT COMPANY— GO ON BATTLE ALERT!

WHAT? WHAT IS IT?!

WHOOSH

HUH?! BUT THE MONITORS SHOW NOTHING...

NO REESPONSE ON PERSONNEL OR INFRARED RADARS.

WHATCHA GOT, NUMBER 5?

YANK

THERE, YOU HEAR THAT? SMOOTH SAILING.

262

FIFTEEN BUGGIES AND EIGHTEEN BIKES, LYING IN AMBUSH AT TWO O'CLOCK. DO YOU *WANT* TO DIE?

UH...

YAHHH!

CALM DOWN, YOU IDIOT!

BRATTA BRATTA

WHERE THEM BANDITS AT?!

WHAP

WHOA!

RED ALERT! RED ALERT!

KCHUNK

AIEE!

ZZ NG

SAFETY RELEASED! ALL UNITS PREPARE FOR BATTLE!

OH, SHIT!
IT REALLY
IS AN
AMBUSH!

?!

DAMN! WE CAN'T STOP IN TIME!

AAAAH! TH' RAILS!!

ALERT, ALERT...

YEOW...

WHAT ABOUT THE OTHERS?

OH, RIGHT... I GOT THROWN OFF FROM THE IMPACT OF THE DERAILING.

DATDATDAT

BOOOM

POP POP

VWEE VWEE

URGH ...

YOU ARE 20 METERS FROM THE TRAIN! RETURN TO YOUR STATION!

THE TRAIN'S OFF THE TRACKS! WE DON'T STAND A CHANCE!

AIEEE!

AAAH! I'M *DONE* WITH THIS!!

YOU HAVE 25 SECONDS TO RETURN, OR YOU WILL BE IDENTIFIED AS A DESERTER AND DETONATED!

TH-THIS IS CRAZY!

....!

I B-BROKE MY L-LEG! AAAH, IT HURTS!

C'MON, HANG IN THERE!

おら!
C'MON!

YORG ?!

W-WAIT UP! HELP!

BRAOOH

HAA AH!

SH-SHIT!

GJAK

10 SECONDS.

NO...MY GUN JAMMED*?!

*Jam: An operation failure that prevents a gun from firing.

NINE.

DRUNNN

AAAAH!!

?!

WH-WHAT?!

THE TRAIN'S NUCLEAR ENGINE IS GONNA BLOW!

R-R-RUN FOR IT!! BAIL OUT!

rait box

BOOM!

EEP!

ALERT, ALERT...

TAKE MY ADVICE: RUN FOR YOUR LIVES!!

*Meltdown: When a nuclear reactor loses cooling control, and the core begins to melt from heat.

AIEEEE! I DON'T WANNA D-D-DIE!

NOT MUCH YOU CAN DO IN THE FACE OF NUCLEAR OBLITERATION.

HEH! I GOT THE WORST LUCK.

YOU'RE NOT ONE OF US MERCENARIES. YOU'RE NOT STUCK HERE.

GO ON AND CLEAR OUT, ALITA.

SHIK

HUPP

AIEE!

TIK
TIK

CLICK

THUMP
ドッ

HEY,
GIVE IT UP!
IT'S GONNA
EXPLODE!!

14

TIK TIK
BEEP TIK

I-I'M LOOSE!

WHO... *ARE* YOU...?!

WH-WHAT...?

JUST SOMEONE WHO MADE A DEAL WITH MEPHISTOPHELES*.

ME...?

FWAP

*__Mephistopheles:__ A capricious demon from Goethe's Faust. By making a deal with the demon, Dr. Faust gains youth and the ability to travel throughout time on a grand adventure.

OOOH!

...

HEH-HEH! Y-YO[U] SAVED MY LIFE TH-THANK YOU THANK YOU!

293

HEH-HEH. WHAT, YOU N-NEVER SEEN A *UFO* BEFORE?

HUH? THAT THERE SHOOTIN' STAR'S MOVIN ALL *FUNNY!*

THEM STARS TONIGHT ARE RIGHT VIVID, I TELL YOU WHAT.

IF Y-YOU'RE GONNA TRY TO H-HIT ON HER, I'D SAVE MY BREATH... AND MY LIFE.

D-DON'T ASK ME.

SAY, WHAT HAPPENED TO ALITA? WHERE'D SHE GO?

I-I'M JUST SAYIN'!

CLANK

SHE SAVED YOUR MISERABLE HIDE, AND YOU'RE STILL GOIN' ON ABOUT THAT STUPID WIVES' TALE?!

THAT OL' OCTOPUS-LIPS!

CARRYING OUT YOUR MISSION IS THE TOP PRIORITY HERE.

WE HAVE BEEN TRACKING DESTY NOVA FOR YEARS AND YEARS...AND WE'VE FINALLY FOUND A CLUE.

YOU MUST GO AND APPREHEND HIM.

IT IS A CERTAINTY THAT NOVA IS BEHIND THE *BARJACK* MOBILE BANDITS.

G.I.B. Director, Bigott Eisenberg

AH!

HEY! WHY DON'TCHA COME DOWN HERE AND EAT?

...ROGER THAT...

I DO.

CARE TO REPEAT THAT?! YOU EXPECT ME TO WALK ACROSS THE WILDERNESS CARRYING A WOUNDED MAN?!

AND I'M NOT TAKING YOU WITH ME. YOU'LL ONLY SLOW ME DOWN.

I HAVE TO LEAVE RIGHT AWAY.

CLANK

GRRR...

COME ON! SHOW ME THE BEST YOU'VE GOT!!

I DON'T CARE IF YOU'RE AN ANGEL OF DEATH OR NOT—I DON'T TAKE KINDLY TO BEIN' OVERLOOKED LIKE THIS!

ALL RIGHT, I'M GAME.

スル SLIP

YOU'RE AWFUL FEISTY FOR A GUY WHO JUST GOT HIS LIFE SAVED.

ドシャッ KSHUD

バチ CLICK

HEH HEH HEH!

I DON'T THINK YOU REALIZE WHAT YOU'VE GOTTEN YOURSELF INTO HERE!

HEH HEH... DON'T ASSUME THAT I'M A PUSHOVER, JUST BECAUSE I AIN'T CYBERIZED, ALITA.

CRUNK

PSHK

ALLOW ME TO SHOW YOU WHAT I CAN DO!

SWISH
Z!!

HEH HEH... IN MY *ANTI-CYBER KOPPO** SCHOOL, WE CALL THAT A "PENETRATION" MOVE!!

HE'S ALL ORGANIC... YET HE CAN USE THE *HERTZA HAUEN?!*

CLANK

I'VE USED THIS LITTLE TRICK TO TAKE DOWN 35 CYBERS SO FAR... AND I WON'T STOP UNTIL I'VE REACHED A THOUSAND!!

THEM CYBERS HAVE TOO MUCH ARMOR TO DEFEAT BARE-HANDED USING NORMAL MEANS! BUT MY PALMS CAN SEND THE IMPACT THROUGH TO THE INSIDE, WHERE IT MAKES A DOWN-RIGHT MESS OF THAT SOFT, JUICY BRAIN!!

---

*Anti-Cyber Koppo: A type of Asian Art. While koppo is said to be one of the oldest forms of martial arts in Japan, going back to Otomo-no-Komaro in the Nara Period (8th century), it was later co-opted and revived by Seiji Horibe for his "Fighting-style Koppo." The word literally means "bone method," but in this case the word "bone" means more like "trick" or "knack," as in, "to have the knack for."

WHAT ARE YOU DOING, A-1? GET MOVING!

!

HEH...

IF HE STANDS IN YOUR WAY, SIMPLY SHOOT HIM!

HEH HEH! WHAT'S WRONG? YOU SEEM FREAKED OUT BY THIS.

WHAT'S WRONG? PENT-UP FRUSTRATIONS?

LISTEN, CONTROL, EVEN I WANT TO BLOW OFF STEAM NOW AND THEN. CUT ME SOME SLACK.

*The conversation between Control and Alita is on an internal line, so Figure Four can't hear them.

THANKS, DIRECTOR BIGOTT.

ALL RIGHT. THREE MINUTES.

...

WHAT CAN I SAY? I'VE GOT A WEAKNESS FOR IDIOTS LIKE THIS GUY.

NOW IT'S TIME TO GIVE YOU MY 100% BEST...

HEH HEH HEH! GUESS I EARNED THAT ONE...

DRIP DRIP

HA HA... WHAT'S WRONG?

IF I'M CLOSE ENOUGH FOR TE-AI, I CAN'T POSSIBLY LOSE!!

I'VE GOT TO GET A STEP CLOSER SO THAT I'M IN PROPER TE-AI* RANGE!

ZIP

RIGHT HERE!!

SWISH

307   *Te-ai: The effective range between combatants for a palm strike. In Koppo, palm attacks stemming from the elbow are effective at an extremely close range. Te-ai range is too close for punches, which originate from the shoulder and cannot reach full power when the target is so close.

HRRG...

TAP TAP

HEH HEH... READY TO GIVE UP YET?

NEVER!!

WHOOSH

HEH HEH HEH! SUPPOSE I HAVE NO CHOICE BUT TO SHOW YOU MY TRUE POWER NOW!!

WELL, I HAVE TO ADMIRE YOUR TENACITY!

STEP!!

THE G-GOD OF LIGHT- NING LOOKS READY TO STRIKE. *BRR*, LORDY...

S-SURE IS *COLD* OUT. I DON'T LIKE THE LOOK OF THIS...

HE B- BETTER NOT BE HAVIN' FUN WITH THAT DEVIL- WOMAN.

A-AND WHAT'S TAKIN' FIGURE SO LONG?

WOBBLE...

HEH HEH HEH! SORRY TO TELL YA, BUT I CAN'T BE BEATEN...

WHY DON'T YOU JUST GIVE UP AND ADMIT DEFEAT?

HEH HEH HEH! YOU'RE ALL... TALK...

WHOMP

HEH HEH! NOT YET!

WHAT THE HELL...? DO I HAVE TO *KILL* YOU TO WIN?

BOOOT

WHAM

MAN... WHAT A CRETIN!

WHEWWW

SLIP

SLIP

THUMP

YAAAAH! THIS FIGHT ISN'T OVER YET!!

SH-SHE'S ALREADY GONE, MAN!

ドッ!! HWAAH

WHAT?! YOU RAN OUT ON ME, ALITA?!

WHAT A H-HEARTLESS BEAST... SHE L-LEFT US OUT HERE IN THE MIDDLE OF NOWHERE...WITH ONLY THE TINIEST BIT OF F-FOOD AND WATER...

ドォロロ VRMMMM

FIGURE FOUR...

WHAT A WEIRDO.

WE'VE GOT SOME EXTREMELY DANGEROUS PATTERNS SHOWING UP ON THE DOPPLER RADAR*.

NOW CLEAR OUT OF THAT ZONE AT ONCE!

...

DID YOU ENJOY YOURSELF, A-1?

I'M SEEING ROTATION BETWEEN THE STRONG UPWARD THRUST AND HEAVY RAIN.

THERE'S A CYCLONE BREWING!!

IT LOOKS LIKE THE EXPLOSION OF STEAM FROM THE NUCLEAR REACTOR AND ITS RESULTING HEAT ARE HITTING THE WESTERN WIND TO FORM A SUPERCELL.

NO...

RADIOACTIVE RAIN?

313

*Doppler radar: Soundwaves change in frequency depending on whether the source is approaching or distancing itself from the listener—this is called the "Doppler effect." A Doppler radar interprets the movement of wind and clouds by calculating from the effect.

316

GET MOV-ING!!

I DON'T NEED YOUR SYMPA—

FIGURE!!

NO THANKS!!

OH...FINE! I'LL DECLINE YOUR SYMPATHY *NEXT* TIME!

UGH, WHAT A LIFE!

THIS IS NO TIME FOR BEING STUBBORN, YOU MORON!

...AND RISK DANGER FOR THE LIVES OF THAT SURFACE TRASH?!

YOU FOOL! YOU...YOU DARE DEFY *MY* ORDERS...

ZALEMITES AREN'T THE ONLY HUMAN BEINGS, DIRECTOR BIGOTT!!

I'VE BEEN HOLDING IT IN ALL ALONG, BUT I'M GIVING YOU A PIECE OF MY MIND TODAY!!

WHO'S GROWING YOUR FOOD, MAKING YOUR CLOTHES, PROCESSING YOUR WASTE, AND SHEDDING BLOOD TO FIGHT FOR YOU?!

S-SILENCE, A-1!

WHO DO YOU THINK MAKES IT POSSIBLE FOR YOU TO LIVE SAFE AND SECURE UP THERE?

AND I'VE HAD ENOUGH OF TAKING ORDERS FROM A COLD-BLOODED MONSTER LIKE YOU!!

WE SURFACE-DWELLERS ARE!!

WE MUST BE CATS, 'CAUSE I RECKON WE GOT US THEM NINE LIVES! I WOKE UP TO FIND WE WERE STUCK RIGHT ON THIS BROKE-DOWN HIGH-RISE...

IF WE'D WAITED ANY LONGER TO LEAVE THAT VEHICLE, WE'D ALL BE SPLATTERED.

HEH HEH HEH! ARE YOU AWAKE, MY SWEET?

HEY, MY HAR-MONICA!

STOP JOKING AROUND AND PULL ME UP!

GYA HA HA!

GUESS WE'VE GOT BETTER LUCK THAN YOU THOUGHT...

"IF YOU GET CLOSE TO ME..."

"...YOU'LL DIE YOUNG!"

I'M NOT GONNA BE YOUR PLAYTHING! YOU UNDER-STAND ME?!

WHOEVER YOU REALLY ARE, I'M TIRED OF THE WAY YOU HELP PEOPLE AND THEN ABANDON THEM WHENEVER IT STRIKES YOUR FANCY!

WHAT ARE YOU SO AFRAID OF?!

C-COME ON, FIGURE...

324

...BUT EVEN FOR A CYBER, A FALL OF THIS HEIGHT WILL HAVE DIRE CONSEQUENCES! SO THINK ABOUT WHAT YOU'VE DONE!!

I'M SURE CUTTIN' THIS WIRE WILL BE CHILD'S PLAY FOR YOU...

UGH...

CONTROL! COME IN, CONTROL!

DAMN, NO SIGNAL...

UNGRATEFUL PUNK... HE HAS NO IDEA WHAT I JUST DID FOR HIM!

TOO BAD! LOOKS LIKE HIS BRAIN MUST HAVE FALLEN OUT AT SOME POINT!

H-HE WASN'T IN THE CAR.

HMM? NOW THAT YOU MEN- TION IT...

HEY! IS *KNUCKLE- HEAD*, THE LEADER OF THOSE BANDITS, STILL INTACT?!

LOOK AT THE SIZE OF THESE RUINS! THERE *MUST* BE SOME FOOD BURIED AROUND HERE!

YOU'VE ALWAYS GOT TO LOOK ON THE POSITIVE SIDE!

M-MAYBE WE'LL FIND SOME FOSSILIZED CANNED FOOD.

YEP, YEP.

SPLISH

I SEE. A VETERAN OF THE DESERT!

EH-HEH... IT'S USUALLY P-PRETTY EASY TO PREDICT WHERE WATER WILL BE.

I WAS W-WORRIED ABOUT RADIO-ACTIVITY, BUT F-FRESH SPRING WATER SHOULD BE SAFE.

SPLASH

プラン PLONG

WHOOOSH

WELL? FEELING APOLOGETIC YET?

スル SHLIP

スル SHLIP

EVEN A CYBER'S GOTTA GET HUNGRY, RIGHT?

HERE, GOT SOME YUMMY CORNED BEEF FOR YA.

I'M SORRY...

FIGURE, LISTEN...

YOU'RE WELL WITHIN YOUR RIGHTS TO BE MAD AT ME.

SO I'LL TELL YOU THE TRUTH.

YOU'RE FROM ZALEM?

I'M A MEMBER OF TUNED—A SERVANT OF ZALEM ON A TOP-SECRET MISSION.

NOPE...

AND I CANNOT DISOBEY THEIR ORDERS...

SOMETIMES I WONDER... WHY I WAS EVEN BORN IN THE FIRST PLACE...

AND IT'S THANKS TO ZALEM THAT I'M ALIVE NOW...

I ONCE READ A PASSAGE IN AN OLD BOOK: "IF YOU WANT TO OWN A SLAVE, YOU EITHER BUY HIM WITH MONEY...OR SAVE HIS LIFE."

AND... WHERE ARE *YOU* FROM?

...MARS? I THINK... I DON'T HAVE ANY MEMORY OF IT.

OHH.

HUH? UH... FROM? I'M FROM...

WHERE'RE YOU FROM?

HEH HEH. MY HOME-TOWN'S A REAL NICE PLACE.

IT'S CALLED ALHAMBRA. IT'S A LITTLE FISHING VILLAGE LOCATED IN AN OLD LAST-CENTURY CITY THAT SANK HALF INTO THE WATER.

EVERY FEW YEARS, A BIG 20-METER SEA SERPENT* WILL WANDER INTO THE BAY LOOKING FOR SEALS.

WE ALL SET OUT IN OUR BOATS AND COMPETE TO SEE WHO'LL LAND THE FIRST HARPOON!

IT'LL RUST YOUR BODY UP.

UGH

I FEEL LIKE I'VE BEEN WANDERING AROUND THE DESERT FOR ALL OF MY LIFE.

THE OCEAN... I'D REALLY LIKE TO SEE THAT SOMEDAY...

あAAAH!ん

HERE! OPEN WIDE!

YOU... TACTLESS CLOD...

*Sea serpent: A marine animal often witnessed, but never scientifically observed. It's said that one once provided as much meat and oil as an entire whale.

YOU'D BETTER HAUL ME UP *RIGHT NOW*, OR YOU'LL NEVER SEE FIGURE FOUR ALIVE AGAIN!

Y-YES?!

YORG!

UM, I H-HEAR YOU LOUD AND CLEAR...

...B-BUT WHAT'S AN INJURED MAN SUPPOSED TO D-DO ALL BY HIMSELF?

B-BUT I CAN'T!

JUST DO SOME-THING!

UGH, HE'S GOT A POINT... DANG.

HRM...

PENETRATED MY TITANIUM-AUGMENTED PALM FROM THAT DISTANCE...

AND DECISIVE ENOUGH TO TAKE THE COUNTER-INITIATIVE IN AN INSTANT! SHE'S NOT ONE OF THE USUAL TRAIN GUARDS!!

TCH!

KRAKK

!

BOOM

GATTA

GATTA

POOSH

BOOM

BOOM

KABOOM

KBLAM

WAHOO!

EEK!

*HV Rounds: High-velocity, small-caliber bullets. After firing, the plastic sabot falls away, increasing penetrating power.

(Side View)

*HSA Rounds: This round has multiple special steel flechettes (needles) inside that launch out of the round and penetrate once the bullet lands. High in stopping power. "High Safety Ammunition."

BOOM

BOOM

BOOM

WHAT IS IT, THEN?!

THE ONLY THING I CAN THINK OF AT THIS CALIBER IS THE HSA* ROUNDS THE BARJACK INDUSTRIAL BUREAU IS DEVELOPING FROM ANCIENT DOCUMENTS...

THE 5.7 MM HV* ROUNDS THE FACTORY'S TRAIN TROOPS USE CAN'T PIERCE THIS ARMOR!

IF THAT'S WHO WE'RE UP AGAINST, WE MUST USE EVERY POSSIBLE MEASURE TO DEFEAT THEM, SERGEANT!!

YESSIR!

WE CAN'T TAKE THEM LIGHTLY. RUMORS ON THE WIND SPEAK OF A ZALEMITE AGENT CALLED THE *ANGEL OF DEATH* WHO'S BEEN SNIFFING AROUND BARJACK ACTIVITIES...

ATTEN-HUT! YOU ARE NOW THE MIGHTIEST SOLDIERS IN THE GALAXY!!

AND NOTHING OUT THERE IS GOING TO STOP YOU!!

GET GOIN', YOU HELL-BEASTS!!

YAAAH! I'M ABOUT TO EXPLODE!

MOVE OUT!

MOVE UP TROOPS ON EITHER SIDE, SO THEY DON'T NOTICE.

YESSIR!

IT'S THE SMALLEST MEN WHO MAKE THE BIGGEST SHOW OF THEIR PRIDE...

IF WE'RE REALLY UP AGAINST ZALEM AGENTS, HE WON'T STAND A CHANCE!

HAH! KNUCKLE'S JUST A DECOY.

I THOUGHT YOU WERE GOING TO SIT BACK UNTIL THE SIGNAL, SIR?

THINK THEY'RE BARJACK, TOO?

THE BOMBARDMENT'S STOPPED...

HFF!

HFF!

AIEEE!

ALL I KNOW IS...

WHO KNOWS? MY COMMUNICATIONS TO ZALEM ARE DAMAGED, SO I HAVE NO INTELLIGENCE SUPPORT. THAT'S HALF OF THE ADVANTAGE OF BEING IN *TUNED*...

HEH... MAN, THIS IS EXCITING.

WE'RE ABOUT TO ENGAGE IN A BATTLE OF LIFE OR DEATH.

GRR!

I W-WANNA GO BACK HOME!

N-N-NO, IT'S NOT... I DON'T WANNA GET STUCK IN A FIREFIGHT!

FLOP.

FLOP.

UH...

HE'S NOT LIKE YOU— HE'S GOT SOMETHING TO LOSE!

YORG'S GOT A WIFE AND KID WAITING FOR HIM TO COME HOME. HAVE SOME CONSIDER- ATION!!

I GUESS I WAS JUST A GUN IN MY PREVIOUS LIFE...

W-WELL... WHATEVER! NOT MY PROBLEM.

TINK

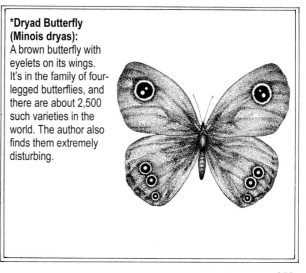

*Dryad Butterfly (Minois dryas): A brown butterfly with eyelets on its wings. It's in the family of four-legged butterflies, and there are about 2,500 such varieties in the world. The author also finds them extremely disturbing.

352

CAPTAIN, IT'S DANGEROUS TO STAND OUT IN THE OPEN.

BUT IT LOOKS COOLER THIS WAY!

I GUESS THEY REALLY *DO* WANT ME TO KILL THEM! WELL, I AIM TO PLEASE!

HAH! WHAT IDIOTS! THEY GAVE AWAY THEIR POSITION!

YEAH, LET'S GO.

PSH! AMATEUR... FORGET HIM.

IGNORE HIM.

SWISH

HEY! I DIDN'T GIVE YOU THOSE ORDERS!!

BOOM

FWIP

YAAH!!

NOT THERE YET!!

MORE! UNTIL EVERYTHING IS BLANK!!

WH-WHAT'S THE MATTER, FIGURE?! LET'S S-SCRAM!!

HUFF!

HUFF!

HOW FAR DOES MY CONCEPT OF "FREEDOM" GO? HOW ROBUST IS IT REALLY?

I ENJOY FREEDOM... AND SO I'VE BEEN PONDERING THE CONCEPT ALL THROUGH MY TRAVELS.

BUT AFTER SEEING THAT LONE WOLF ALITA, I RECKON THAT AIN'T NECESSARILY THE ONLY WAY.

UNTIL NOW, I'VE BELIEVED THAT SOLI-TUDE WAS THE WAY TO FREEDOM...

FREEDOM'S CONTROLLIN' THE RUDDER TO YOUR OWN SHIP.

SO I'M GOING BACK!!

Y-YOU FOOL! NO ONE'S HERE TO SEE YOU A-ACT LIKE A HERO!!

THEY'RE M-MONSTERS! LET THEM HAVE THEIR W-WAR! WE DON'T NEED ANY PART OF IT!!

WH-WHAT?! FIGURE FOUR!!

CLANK CLANK

JUST FIND SOMEWHERE TO HIDE FOR NOW.

...ULP?!

TUG

D-DON'T LEVE ME BEHIND HERE, MAN!!

YOU'RE DEAD MEAT!!

HAH!

STOP RIGHT THERE, WILDCAT!

WE'VE SEEN ENOUGH EVIDENCE TO ACKNOWLEDGE YOUR EXTRA-ORDINARY COMBAT PROWESS!

BUT IF YOU BUDGE EVEN AN INCH FROM THAT SPOT, THIS 30-MM CHAIN GUN WILL TURN YOU INTO BOLOGNESE!

GYA HA HA!

GWA HAW HAW!

BWA HA HA!

EEE HEE HEE!

YOU'LL LIVE ANOTHER DAY NOW, KNUCKLE.

WH-WHY, COLONEL?! I DIDN'T CALL FOR BACKUP!!

WOBBL

WHAP WHAP

HYACK HYACK HYACK!

GRR... YOU USED ME AS A *DECOY!!*

WHO'S A LUCKY BOY, HUH?

FFFH!

FFFH!

FFFH!

THERE'S NO RUSH! HER BRAIN HOLDS INTELLIGENCE VALUE.

I CAN'T HOLD BACK ANY-MORE!!

SHLURP

I...I...I WANT TO SHOOT HER!!

WHEN DID THEY SET UP A TRAP?!

RATATAT

BLAM BLAM

MORE ENEMIES TO THE REAR?!

BOOOM

AAAH!

*SPIDEY:

One of the special TUNED armaments. It's a Zalem-designed insectoid robot bomb that is programmed to set up traps according to the terrain. It can also be commanded externally, allowing for a wide array of tactical uses.

(When stored)

FIRE!

BWEEE

FUMP

MISSILE BEES!

SHAK

BIP

TAKKA TAKKA

VWEEE

BIP

*MISSILE BEE:

One of the special TUNED armaments, a bee-shaped cyborg missile. It has a "fire-and-forget" auto-aiming capability, and can snipe with incredible accuracy.

...BY THE *ANGEL OF DEATH!!*

SO THIS IS WHAT THEY MEAN...

W-WAIT, ALITA!

HAAAA!

HA HA HA...
A FRIEND IN NEED IS A FRIEND INDEED, YORG.

H-HEH HEH...

THUMP

PLIP PLIP

UGH...

CLIKK

BOOM

BOOM

BOOM

BOOM

BOOM

YORRRG!!

"BOILING METAL"
HEAVY TROOPERS

FIG-UURE!!

FIGHT_034 Land of Betrayal

...UNG...

GAKK

YORG...!

AH...

AAH...

SHIVER SHIVER

SHIVER

BRING OUT THE RESTRIC- TORS!

THUD

CANK

AUUGH!

BZZAT

BRING UP THE REAR GUARD AND LET'S RESUPPLY AS PLANNED!!

SOUND OFF AND GET OUR NUMBERS!

HUFF!

HUFF!

...

PFAH...

"FREEDOM'S CONTROLLING THE RUDDER TO YOUR OWN SHIP..."

I'M S-SORRY ABOUT THIS, FIG- URE...

"YORG'S GOT A WIFE AND KID WAITING FOR HIM TO COME HOME. HAVE SOME CONSIDER- ATION!!"

C-COLONEL BOZZLE!

WHAT ARE YOU DOING HERE, YORG?

GLUG

387

HEH! YOU KNOW WHAT THEY SAY... "IF YOU CAN'T BEAT 'EM, JOIN 'EM!"

L-LISTEN, I KNOW YOU'RE A PROUD DESCENDENT OF THE G-GREEN BERETS*, AND USED TO LEAD A M-MERCENARY GROUP OF YOUR OWN...

...B-BUT I HEARD YOU DIED IN BATTLE AGAINST BARJACK TWO YEARS AGO...

I HAD COME FACE-TO-FACE WITH THE GRAND AMBITIONS OF THE GREAT LEADER *DEN!!*

UNTIL I ACTUALLY FACED OFF AGAINST THEM, I THOUGHT BARJACK WAS JUST SOME SILLY BANDIT STARTUP... BUT I REALIZED MY MISTAKE ONCE I LOST!

...THROW OFF THE YOKE OF ZALEM, AND CREATE A NATION OF OUR OWN FOR THE SURFACE-DWELLERS!!

WE WILL BURN THE FACTORY FLAT, BRING THE SKY TO EARTH...

*Green Berets: Referring to the special elite force of the American military. In this era, it seems to be considered the name of some powerful tribe of ancient warriors.

THEN QUIT WASTING TIME AND PACK UP!

Y-YES, SIR, AS ORDERED...

HEY, WALNUT-BRAIN! DID YOU GET 'EM OILED UP?!

ゴゴゴ… RMMBB

VRRMMM

ゴォォ—— RRMMMBB

ゴ
グ
ッ
GLUG

ゴ
キ
ュ
ッ
GULK

ゴ
キ
ュ
ッ
GULK

EVEN
BULLETS
ARE SO
SCARED
THAT THEY
AVOID ME!!

BWAAH!
BACK TO
LIFE!

GET UP!!

UNG!

HEH! JUST LIKE YORG SAID, THIS DRYAD BUTTERFLY DID THE TRICK.

LOOKS LIKE SHE'S OUT COLD.

YOU'LL GET YOUR FULL INTERROGATION ONCE WE REJOIN THE MAIN FORCE...

...BUT I HAVE TWO OR THREE QUESTIONS TO ASK BEFORE THEN.

RISE AND SHINE, LITTLE ANGEL OF DEATH...

I SUSPECT... THAT MEANS... THEY'VE CUT ME LOOSE FROM THE *TUNED* PROGRAM...

IT'S BEEN OVER 48 HOURS SINCE I LOST CONTACT WITH ZALEM...

48... HOURS...

WHAT?!

BUT ON THE OTHER HAND...IF WE'RE GOING TO JOIN THE MAIN BARJACK FORCE, THEN PERHAPS...

I HAVE NO HOPE LEFT. FIGURE FOUR IS DEAD, AND NOW THEY WILL SURELY DEFILE MY BRAIN BEFORE THEY FINALLY KILL ME...

OOOH!

SMIRK ニヤリ

PROFESSOR NOVA? THAT KOOKY STRATE-GIST?

HE'S CHIEF DEN'S FAVORITE. I SEE...

MY PRIMARY MISSION IN TUNED WAS TO CAPTURE THE ESCAPED ZALEMITE SCIENTIST, DESTY NOVA...

WHO'S IDO...?

A ZALEMITE DOCTOR WHO WORKS FOR NOVA.

AND THE ONLY REASON I'M IN TUNED IS SO I CAN SEE DAISUKE IDO, WHO NOVA TOOK AWAY FROM ME!!

HA-HAAA! I'M GETTIN' YOU OUTTA HERE, ALITA!!

NO, YOU IDIOT! DON'T!!

KRUNCH

SHUT UP! WHAT'S WRONG WITH YOU?! BAWLING AND WAILING LIKE A LITTLE CHILD!

IS THIS THE SAME ANGEL OF DEATH THAT STRUCK SUCH TERROR IN ME?! HAVE YOU NO *SHAME*?!

HOW CAN YOU DO THIS TO ME?! I WAS FINALLY ABOUT TO SEE IDO!!

IDOOO!!

WHONK

THE COLONEL'S BEEN SHOT!

MOBILIZE THE SOCKETEERS!

HEY, WHAT'S WRONG WITH THEM?!

BLUB

BLUB

RATTLE

PSSST

ADRENAL-IZER!

BING

TSSK

WHAT?!

I REFILLED ALL THOSE SYRINGES WITH CLEANING SOLUTION.

GUH... GLUG...

BLUB

BLUB

HAAAA!

DIE!!

YOU TURNED TRAITOR ON US, WALNUT-BRAIN!!

HAHAAA! I SABOTAGED ALL OF YOUR GUNS!!

AAH!

DON'T BE MISTAKEN... I JUST DIDN'T WANT THOSE OTHER SCUM-BAGS TO KILL YOU *FIRST...*

HAAAA! I'VE REALLY BEEN LOOKING FORWARD TO THIS!!

CLICK

FIGHT_035 Rain Maker

BARJACK WAS JUST A TITLE—AN EASY BANNER TO STAND BENEATH...

YOU SEE, ALL I REALLY NEED IN LIFE IS TO DESTROY MACHINES AND FIRE GUNS! I DON'T CARE WHO MAKES THAT POSSIBLE!!

FWIP

?!

SHUK

THIS IS A 28-MM HE* ROUND, CAPABLE OF PIERCING 10 CENTIMETERS OF SOLID ARMOR!!

BUT THERE'S ONLY ONE SHOT!

G'CHAK

*HE ROUND (HIGH EXPLOSIVE)

(SIDE VIEW)

The front of a shaped-charge explosive is hollowed conically, so that when it hits the target, all of the energy is focused and directed toward the point of the cone, utilizing a property called the Munroe effect. The penetrating effect of the HE round is roughly proportional to the diameter of the shell.

GIVE ME YOUR BEST, ALITA!!

COME!

IT FEELS **GOOD** TO LOSE CONTROL, DOESN'T IT?! YOU WANT TO BE NOTHING BUT ANOTHER NAMELESS, LONE BEAST, JUST RACING THROUGH THE WILDERNESS AS FAR AS YOU CAN GO!!

WE ARE MUCH ALIKE... I COULD SENSE IT LIKE A BOLT OF LIGHTNING WHEN WE FIRST MET! HA HAAAA!

HA...

THEN LET'S VENTURE FORTH TOGETHER, INTO THAT BLANK SHEET OF THE WORLD— A WORLD OF TOTAL FREEDOM!!

HA! HA-HA!

DRIP DRIP

HEH HEH... I THINK I'VE GOTTEN MUCH BETTER WITH THIS HARMONICA!

WHAP WHAP

I DON'T BELIEVE IT! YOU'RE *ALIVE*, YOU DOLT!

OW! OW!

HERE'S YOUR HAR-MONICA BACK. SORRY 'BOUT ALL THE SCRATCHES.

NO...IT'S YOURS NOW.

WHOAH!!

SO KNUCKLE'S DEAD...

EVEN THE INSECTS HAVE SOULS AND FEELINGS, AS THEY SAY... IT IS THE SHAME OF A LIFETIME THAT I FAILED TO HEED THE WARNING SIGNS IN HIS DEMEANOR!!

NOTHING CAN BE ALLOWED TO STAND IN THE WAY OF THE REALIZATION OF OUR LOFTY IDEALS— NOT EVEN A BUG!

KILL THEM!

YORG!

Y...

TWITCH

TWITCH

F-FORGIVE ME...FIGURE, ALITA... FORGIVE ME...

I'M...I'M NO GOOD, TOO WEAK...A-AND NOW I DON'T EVEN H-HAVE THE RIGHT TO SEE MY W-WIFE AGAIN. J-JUST...JUST...

YORG...!

HRNG

FIGURE
...

WHAT...?

*Soft machine: While it originally was a euphemism for the human body, in this context it refers to a machine constructed from the nanomolecular level up, using molecular engineering.

WHOOOSH

DSHHH

WHAP

OUCH!

HAH! HA HA HA! IT'S RAIN!!

FSHAAA

FWIP

WH-WHAT'S *THAT?!*

FWAP

I DID NOTHING...

DID YOU PERFORM SOME KIND OF WEATHER MANIPULATION, DIRECTOR?

WHAT IS THIS...?

THEN I SUPPOSE YOU LOST, DIRECTOR.

I WAS MERELY OBSERVING OUT OF CURIOSITY AS TO HOW ALITA'S LIFE WOULD CLOSE THE BOOK ON HER STUBBORN REBELLIOUS-NESS.

DO YOU BELIEVE IN FATE AND MIRACLES?

DR. RUS-SELL...

...

GO AND RESCUE THEM.

Battle Angel Alita Part 6: Rain Maker / END

The Factory Trading System